Farrakhan Speaks

Title: Farrakhan Speaks

ISBN-13: 978-1-942825-33-3

Author: Kambiz Mostofizadeh

Publisher: Mikazuki Publishing House

Copyright: 2020. All Rights Reserved.

Description: This book explores the ideas of Louis Farrakhan of the Nation of Islam.

Notice: No part of this work may be reproduced or transmitted in any form or by any means electronic or mechanical including photocopying recording or by any information storage and retrieval system without written permission from the publisher. The publisher and author accept no responsibility for your actions based on this book. This book is for entertainment purposes only. If the Mikazuki Publishing House™ book is not available place a request with any bookstore to order it for you. Mikazuki Publishing House™ is a book publisher that started in 2011 in Los Angeles California. The Mikazuki Publishing House™ Trademark is protected by the United States Patent Trade Organization Trademark Registration Number 4323734.

I0039129

Farrakhan Speaks

Louis Farrakhan on Zimbabwe

We were in Zimbabwe. In Zimbabwe where the President is President Mugabe. Mugabe is the about the only one in Africa that stood up with strength. May Allah be pleased with him and give him even longer life to trouble the West. But in Harari, the number one industry was building coffins. 5,000 Africans were dying each week, 20,000 a month. From what? Aids. I was a guest of the Ministry of Health and when we were at luncheon they were bragging that every child in Zimbabwe had been vaccinated. The man that is your former slavemaster, you trust him to put a needle in your arm? Though the Tuskegee experiment should have shown you. Have you forgotten? Have you become that

Farrakhan Speaks

stupid and insensitive? You say you are too big for hate. You are a damn fool. You are not bigger than God and God hates. God removes entire nations from the earth that He don't like. You are just a coward! You hate your Mother when she don't give you what you want, you hate your Father, you kill your brother!!!! Why are people dying in the ghetto? Because you love? No because you hate!!! But your hate is unintelligent!.

Louis Farrakhan on Libya

Where were you in Rwanda? Where are you in the Congo? Why did you go to Darfur? Because oil is there. You don't want to save the Libyan

Farrakhan Speaks

people. That is your noble motive to hide your wicked agenda. I want to warn you in the name of Allah, that this is more complex than what you think. Go in to Libya if you want to. The Libyans do not want foreign occupation on their land. If you are not careful you will unite the Libyan people against you. Qaddafi has not been sitting in a tent twiddling his thumbs. This man has been investing in African development. This man has been moving throughout Africa. This man has friends all over the world. He may not be your friend. What did you do in Waco? What did you do when your people rose up? They had weapons you bombed them. What did you do in Philadelphia with the M.O.V.E. movement? Did you talk them out of their home or did you bomb

Farrakhan Speaks

them? We didn't hear any outcry from you religious hypocrites that love the lives of humans beings. (Obama) you are liar and hypocrite and I warn my brother don't you let these wicked demons move you in a direction that will absolutely ruin your future with your people in Africa and throughout the world. You can't order him (Qaddafi) to step down and get out. Who the hell do you think you are? That you can talk to a man that built a country over 42 years and ask him step down and get out. Can anybody ask you? Well there is a lot now going to ask you to step down and get out because they don't want no Black face in the White House. Be careful how you handle this situation because it is coming to America it has

Farrakhan Speaks

already started. Look at what is going on in your own country. Remember your words because the American people are rising against their government. It is not Muslims, it is not Black people. It is White militia and they are angry with their government and they are well armed. Are you going to tell them to lay down their arms and lets talk it over peacefully? I hope so, but if not America will be bathed in blood. Not because Farrakhan said so, but because the dissatisfaction in America has reached the boiling point. Be careful how you manipulate the dissatisfaction in Libya and in other parts of the Muslim world.

Farrakhan Speaks

Louis Farrakhan on Mystery Babylon

This mystery Babylon, the Honorable Elijah Muhammad teaches us, is the United States of America. Her influence is all over the world. And she has spread her filth and abomination in every nation of the earth and all the nations have drunk of the wine of committing fornication with America. Yes it is true. It is unfortunate that it is true. That America's environment is so foul that it has become the natural place for anyone that wants to rebel against submission to the will of God. America leads the world in alcohol consumption, drug consumption, murder, violence, and rape. America has more of her citizens in prison than any nation on the earth. In every major or minor city, you can see men

Farrakhan Speaks

who are in love with and worship the same sex, men. And women worshipping their own sex. It has gotten so bad that little boys and girls in the schools are practicing homosexuality and lesbianism. And there is no shame because the country, the country is so foul that it has allowed every rebellious devil to find a place in America. Live as you please, do as you please. It is pretty terrible that you don't know where to send your children to school. It is pretty rough that right now in the jails that the practice of homosexuality and lesbianism is going on everyday. So when the brothers and sisters come out of prison, and the girlfriend don't know that he is become something different. He is a man by day and something else by night. He is

Farrakhan Speaks

on the downlow. Sodom and Gomorah look like a kindergarden compared to the United States of America. So the Bible teaches that smoke of her burning will be seen afar off. And the nations that committed fornication with her, will wail and mourn because of her fall.

Louis Farrakhan on the Dollar

In 1917 America got involved in the first World War and in order to fight that war America had to borrow money and that's when the debt started. Because when she borrowed money she had to borrow it from somewhere. Federal Reserve print have money printed, you borrow it, you pay the expenditures of war and all you

Farrakhan Speaks

bought was paper. But this paper has interest attached to it, even though it's based on nothing. Just try to follow me. Don't go to sleep. You've been asleep for four hundred years. It's time to wake up. After World War 1 They wanted to draw America into World War Two. It was a European thing, Hitler and the boys. But in order for America to get involved in World War II in Europe, she had to borrow more money during the debt started escalating. Then Japan attacked and America borrowed more money and more money. She borrowed in 1933. America went off the gold standard. So there was nothing after 1933 to back this so after that was nothing. And in 1971 it was completed. No more goal. And in the 70s, you could buy an

Farrakhan Speaks

ounce of gold for $35 an ounce. I was with the honorable Elijah Muhammad one day and he pulled out a gold coin and put it on the table and he said in the future, this would be the medium of exchange because the paper will lose its value. I want to quickly show how the debt has climbed. After World War II and the Korean War, everytime America went to war she had to borrow money. There was a time when America would borrow money from her own citizens and they were used to buy war bonds. We used to buy treasury bonds and securities that we would keep in a safe for our children and they would say in five years or in 10 years you can cash this bond in and you will get this plus interest you remember that. But today, Fifty-two percent

Farrakhan Speaks

of America's burgeoning debt is owned by

Foreign governments. So it ain't no more that

we could sell bonds to our citizens. We sell

bonds to China, we sell bonds and securities to

Japan. We sell bonds and securities to Great

Britain. Let me show you. Who owns what? This

kind of stuff is classroom stuff. But every time

you come to this house, it'll be a classroom.

According to this pie graph, Intragovernmental

debt is three trillion 794 billion The publicly held

debt Which is still government responsibility to

trillion 674 billion. But the publicly he'll

foreigners death. Rather than America alms. His

two trillion 240 billion dollars The Japanese

have bought up 649 billion dollars of American

bonds and securities. Plus they have one point

Farrakhan Speaks

two trillion dollars in foreign currency reserves.
The largest currency reserves in the world is in
China. You see why America would jump on
Cuba a communist country 90 miles away and
talk sweet to China a communist country
because China got America by the testicles. I
use that language because every male in here
knows how painful that is. The Chinese in bonds
and securities 354 billion, the British 249 billion,
OPEC as the oil producing countries a hundred
and two billion, Korea sixty six billion, Taiwan 63
billion, the Caribbean Banks 63 billion, Germany
56 billion, Hong Kong 55 billion, Brazilians 54
billion, Canadians 49 billion, Luxembourg 38
billion, Mexico 36 billion, the French 31 billion,
Singapore 29 billion, Swiss 27 billion, the Turks

Farrakhan Speaks

24 billion, the Swedes 19 billion, the Irish 19 billion, the Dutch 18 billion, the Thai 17 billion, the Israelis 17 billion, the Belgians 15 billion, the Indians 15 billion, the Italians 14 billion, the Polish 13 billion, and all others a hundred and forty eight billion. Now when you go and put turn on the news and you find out that China has some American ports. How did that happen the Arabs got so much and so much the Chinese got? Well, I read that even on I-90. On the toll booth area. That has been sold to Spain. Wait, wait, wait, wait, wait when America borrows all this money all over the world. She's the largest borrower of all the nations in the earth. Almost combined. Look at this now. When you owe a lot of money, sometimes in order to get some

Farrakhan Speaks

money back to pay your liabilities you sell off

your assets. Look family. I just want to come

straight to you the aggregate wealth or worth of

3,000 by 2,000 miles continental United States

of America is 41 to 50 trillion dollars. All the

federal buildings that are in America and all over

the world are 1.26 trillion. All these people that

America owes, suppose they say well wait a

minute. American not doing too good. We want

to call the debt. Now, let's take this up to the

government of the United States. In 2006

America posted a deficit of 450 billion dollars

How did she get a deficit? She gets revenue

from taxing. Excise taxes, tariffs, and taxes on

corporations trade. She builds her Revenue

base. All the money that came into the treasury

Farrakhan Speaks

last year. Was not enough to equal what she

had budgeted for that year and the money that

America took in in taxes. Couldn't even pay the

interest on what she already owed. So this

money is called a Federal Reserve Note. They

have United States currency. You see it in red.

But the Federal Reserve Note is in green. And

they make sure they get that red one back.

Yeah, you got a note. This is not created by

wealth creation. This is created by debt. So the

more debt America owes, the more the Federal

Reserve gives the engraving corporation

instructions to print more money and the more

money that they put in circulation the weaker the

dollar becomes because there's nothing backing

this dollar but the gross national product of

Farrakhan Speaks

America. The symbolic value of America and the
military might of America. That's what backs the
dollar. The debt of America, the national debt
they said last year December Was 8 trillion.
Eight hundred billion dollars increasing at a
billion and a half dollars a day. That's the
national debt. But I read something. Sent to me
by my wonderful research team. That If you're in
a corporation, you can't have two sets of books.
practices It's and debt that they show the public
is not the real debt of the country. Say last year
alone. The dead that they showed us in 2005 as
370 billion. Would have been seven hundred
and sixty billion if the if it were the audited set of
books and then even with that set of books if
they figured in Medicare. Social Security some

Farrakhan Speaks

of the other Pension funds and stuff the dead would have been three and a half trillion dollars. Now is some young boys in here young girls. You get a job you pay into the social security so that when you reach 65 years of age, you start collecting benefits. Sorry. By the time you get this on. Ain't going to be nothing there for you. They going to take as much as they can from your salary. And they're betting that you won't reach 65. And most of our young men Don't reach 65. I'm almost finished. No brothers and sisters. We all are the victims of something that happened in this country. That violates the Constitution The Constitution declares That only Congress Can have the right to Mint money? And produce bonds and securities. That's an act

Farrakhan Speaks

of Congress. But in 1913. On the 23rd day of December, a group of international bankers who wanted control of the money of America with the help of US senators and the US President passed the Federal Reserve Act which brought in the Federal Reserve Bank. Now when you say Federal Reserve you think that Federal means it's owned by the government. Federal Express is not the government. And the Federal Reserve is not the US government. It is a group of international Bankers Jews and gentiles who are correctly called in the Book of Revelation the Synagogue of Satan. They have gained control. I want you to hear me. Gained control and set up a Central Bank in America that is not controlled by the US Congress. And in 1913 the

Farrakhan Speaks

16th Amendment of the Constitution was ratified which gives the government the authority to tax the people. Up to 1913 America's debt was controlled by the American citizens and America was solvent in 1913. She didn't owe nothing. In 1862 Abraham Lincoln imposed income tax on the citizens to pay for the Civil War. Ten years later in 1872 the income tax was repealed. But in 1894 Congress tried to bring it back and the Supreme Court said it was unconstitutional. But in 1913 when the Federal Reserve Act was passed in Congress the IRS was re-enacted because the Federal Reserve was going to put America in debt and you the citizen or so-called citizen would have to pay for America's debt through taxation.

Farrakhan Speaks

Louis Farrakhan Speech in Chicago

So every day there's some killing. Senator Kirk, Senator Durbin saying we going to raise millions of dollars from Congress because we got to go to Chicago and we're going to arrest 18,000 Gangster Disciples. They already got the prisons and the concentration camps ready. The former Police chief in Chicago and the Black officers came to have lunch with me at the National House and the black officers were talking to me about good Community Police relations. Yes, and it sounded real good and certainly as a man that wants to see our people safe I said that sounds good. But then I said this

Farrakhan Speaks

train is running on two tracks. But in the other track you ain't say nothing about. Now I want to talk about that track. I said, I read that you ordered 17,000 automatic rifles with hollow-point bullets armor piercing bullets for your police. Did I make a mistake today? Did I read something incorrectly? No. I said well tell me what are you expecting? That you would arm your police like that, and I said, you know Superintendent or Chief and said how I also read that most of the police departments in the major cities are being trained by Blackwater, which is a mercenary group that they use in Iraq and they are training police. Did you hear me? Now the police forces are being given weapons that are only used in military theaters of War. So when you see the

Farrakhan Speaks

police armed like they are, that's not to Serve and Protect, that is to kill. I don't know whether you have that picture upstairs of the group. That is the military force that came against the people in Missouri. Could you show it? When I saw that come up. I looked in the faces of those police and you could see the hate in their eyes and one of them was standing there saying Bring It On. They have a desire to kill us wholesale. Now Chicago is going to be the epicenter of what they're about to. Do. You know why? Because I'm here, Reverend Jackson is here. Black Consciousness is here. They are already here but they're increasing their numbers working with the police tactical forces and they want to work in the hood with gangs. Well what

Farrakhan Speaks

is it all about? Now look at the money that's
been given to rappers. To continue to drill kind
of rap. This is the hardest core rap that there is.
It is killing killing killing drugs guns whores
disrespect of our women and because they give
you money and contracts that will allow you to
put gold in your teeth and bling bling around
your neck. And then you can come back into
Hood riding expensive cars. But your brothers
and sisters are dying on your words? And you
are aiding in the conspiracy to exterminate the
black male. Now I will tell you what I want you to
do. What you got to know is that at the highest
levels of government they've plotted our demise
and to come into Chicago with heavy Armament
to make Chicago the example. Perhaps during

Farrakhan Speaks

that time, you know, maybe go after arrest
Farrakhan and the Muslims and shut this thing
down because we're the only man standing
because they did compromise everybody else.
But I want to tell you. We're not going to run
from this because if you plan the slaughter of
Black people in America starting with a
Slaughter in Chicago, let me tell you what you
can expect. I see that you know that I've been
telling you about this. Quit what is getting worse
now because you getting worse in your plans. If
you my brothers and don't change and Don't
Stop The Killing of each other then the wrath of
God will descend and blood will be seen in the
gutters of Chicago, but it'll be your blood our
blood but then God will answer swiftly. You are

Farrakhan Speaks

the people of God, but you are acting like agents of the devil and that has to stop. This is the greatest audience that I will have ever spoken to. Because it is these young people that are the hope, but they're in the crosshairs of Destruction.

Louis Farrakhan on UFO's

On those planes, each plane, 1500 of them have three bombs. The wheel has two natures. When those bombs hit the earth, there's a drill. And it'll go down into the Earth one mile and bring up a mountain one mile high destroying everything in a 50 square mile radius. How do those planes know about your military

Farrakhan Speaks

installations? You've caught them over all the military installations, not only here but in England in France in Germany in Russia and China in India. You want to know where they come from? Um, you want to you want to give the credit to somebody from outer space? Hell no they not from outer space. You are a baby White folks in your knowledge of science. We only gave you one book of higher mathematics and you built a great world, but there are 59,999 more. So that's why your scientist said they are faster than our technology by a million years. They made from here from the finest steel. Oh, man, they fly at speeds. They clocked him at 9,000 and more. Those people are the Angels. They're up there. They know what you think and

Farrakhan Speaks

before you can execute they know it. These are

the people from God. Now they asked why is

the government keeping it a secret? They kept

asking that over and over this morning. Well, let

me tell you. L Ron Hubbard In his book on

radiation said whenever there's a weapon that a

nation has no defense against, that nation's

sovereignty is threatened because it is the duty

of every nation to protect its citizens. So when

America developed the hydrogen Bomb the

atom bomb and this high technology weaponry

and Russia did both of them, it made all the

smaller Nations feel frightened. And so each of

them had a camp. In the camp of Russia or in

the camp of America, right? That weapon is so

powerful. The angels on that human-built planet

Farrakhan Speaks

know how to make a wall out of air and that's
why the Bible said behold the day cometh that
shall burn as an oven.. These people have no
weapons to fight God. Heat that can cause
buildings to come down. That wheel has been
up there since 1929 and it has bothered nobody.

There's another part to that wheel, the New
Jerusalem. Up there everything we got down
here. They got it up there. But it's perfectly pure
and the wisdom to purify. The planet is there to
heal all disease is there now. I'm very public
with you about my condition. Most leaders don't
want to talk about what they've been through.
Now you all know all about my illness because I

told it all. What did Paul mean when he said I
have kept the faith, I have fought the good fight,
I have finished my course and now is laid up for
me a crown of righteousness and I go. That that
great judge of righteousness will keep that
crown and is not only for me but it's for us who
loved his appearance, I came here tonight to tell
you that there is one more thing that I had to do.
I started the process of doing it today. They'll be
angry with me. And I will be betrayed into their
hands. Jesus was a good man, but they
charged him with blasphemy and then they
charged him with sedition. I'm ready to do
whatever God has for me to do. I'm on my way
to my Father, but I will return a new man. Not
now. Allah will never reveal the new wisdom

Farrakhan Speaks

while the wicked have power. So when you hear that the Minister is gone and some of you will see me go. They said they saw him go up in a cloud. If you come back in like manner when you see me again, I'll be a new man. Who are you? When you see me again. I can show you my sides that have been pierced. When it took my organs, Doctors thought they would get rid of me. But I'm alive and when you see me again, you know that I've been in the presence of God. And that's where you are going. You are God's people and you can decide whether you want to do righteousness or whether you want to stay in the condition that you're in. But I'm telling you when I finish this lecture today, God is going to answer what I said. You see the

Farrakhan Speaks

wheels over the major cities and the

chastisement is going to increase and there will

be earthquakes in America like you saw in Haiti

like you saw in Chile. Like there was in Japan.

You're going to have to learn Emergency

Management. You don't know how to protect

your life. You don't know what to do when

disaster strikes. If Haiti had been more prepared

lives could have been saved. Now I say to our

President. Just watch and if God answers then

He is answering me so that you can submit that

your people are suffering. You can't ease their

plight, but you can use your bully pulpit. Speak

for the poor. Yes, speak for the weak. Yes

speak for those the working class. For any one

of the White people that voted for you are not

Farrakhan Speaks

going to turn you down because you spoke up

for the least among us. You can do it. And by

the way, Mr. President, I know, Mr. Buchanan

said they spent 40 trillion dollars on Negroes

and they haven't produced no results. You're

right. You can. See you never spent it helping

the rightly guided civilized man. If you want to

ease up what's happening in America then help

me. I know you've helped Israel for 60 years

with no results because the real children of

Israel are us. The Christian right? You got it

wrong. You want to help Israel? I ask you to

look at the transatlantic slave trade. I asked you

to look at what we've done. We've fought we

bled we died for this country. And if you would

turn back some of our tax dollars. Troubled

Farrakhan Speaks

asset relief program for us. You can't talk about reparations. But we can't stop talking about it. Put some money in back of us. Look at the product we produced. We can reform our people. We can civilize our people. We can go into the prisons and change them up and in helping Susan Taylor and mentoring programs. We can make a better people but we need help. Now is your turn.

Louis Farrakhan on Ezekiel's Wheel

The Honorable Elijah Muhammad saw a dreadful looking plane in the sky. He said it was a man-made mechanical object. A half a mile by a half a mile and in it were 1500 little planes.

Farrakhan Speaks

Made like the sphere of spheres in the universe but these are little wheels that Ezekiel saw 595 BC. He had a vision of a wheel in the middle of a wheel in the middle of the air that was a cloud by day and a pillar of Fire by Night. Listen. And now the wheel that Ezekiel saw that Master Farad Muhammad pointed out to The Honorable Elijah Muhammad around 1931 is a reality that is being talked about by governments and Scholars and scientists all over the world. They call them UFO's. They're not from another planet brothers and sisters. They're not Aliens. They are human beings just like you with superior wisdom to the wisdom of this world. Listen, that's why the government of America that calls it top secret. Cannot bring itself to

Farrakhan Speaks

admit that there's another Power. That there's more wisdom. Greater than any wisdom that he has. And this sphere of spheres that is up above our heads, he has no power to defeat it. It is there for two reasons; one is the destruction of the wicked and two is the planting of a brand new civilization.

Louis Farrakhan on Elijah Muhammad

I was speaking to the Honorable Elijah Muhammad about a lecture that I had given and in that lecture, I compared the oft-repeated prayer of the Muslims called the al-fatiha with the oft-repeated prayer of the Christians, which is called The Lord's Prayer. And as I was delineating my understanding of these two great

Farrakhan Speaks

prayers, he said to me Yes, brother. And you may sit as the father over the house when I am gone. I didn't fully understand the meaning of his words, but when he said you may sit as the father he was telling me that when he was gone. and that I would sit in his with the authority and the power of his seat over the house and the house represented 40 million or more black people in America and four billion, four hundred million black brown and red people over our planet and it even included the Caucasian as well. So I'm going to speak to you today as a father. I will speak to you my beloved brothers and sisters but I will speak to the president of the United States and the government of the United States of America. I will speak to the

Farrakhan Speaks

Kings and the rulers of the world. I will speak to the pope and to the religious leaders because you have to know that your time has come. And so here's how I desire to guide you. And to warn us of things that are coming that you must try to prepare yourselves for we are absolutely living in the change of worlds. The Honorable Elijah Muhammad once said I am the richest man alive because God has given to me a nation. And he was not just speaking of the original people in America. He was speaking of that Nation because in the end which is right now, there won't be many nations. They will only be one nation under God. All other kings listen all other rulers soon all other governments all other flags will be done away with and those who

Farrakhan Speaks

survive what is coming. Notice those who survive what is coming, you will be living in that which is called the Hereafter and the Hereafter means here on this Earth after the destruction of the power of this present Wicked World to dominate the lives of the people of our planet. My Christian pastors, to my nationalist brothers and sisters, to Muslims all over the world and to you my beloved brothers and sisters I have been before you as a student of the honorable Elijah Muhammad for now 54 years. No, just listen. In 1981, after being underground for 41 months gathering people to help in the rebuilding of Elijah Muhammad's work we had our first saviors day of this new dispensation at the auditorium theater here in Chicago. And at

Farrakhan Speaks

that time I mentioned to the world that the man
Elijah Muhammad that we all thought was dead
was very much alive. When I made that
statement I knew there would be a falling away
from me because I and we some of us had seen
a body. And there was a death certificate. There
was a funeral. The minister was saying to the
world that Elijah Muhammad was indeed alive.
Some thought that the minister was an
incredible liar. That I had lost my mind and
some who were in the ministry under my
leadership had walked away and many of my
nationalist friends walked away from me
because they could not understand how I could
stand before the world and say that a man that
the world believed was dead was actually alive.

Farrakhan Speaks

One of my very dear friends a lawyer who had been with me from the beginning of my effort to rebuild his work, attorney Lou Myers, came to my house after that lecture and we went to a little restaurant and he said why did you say that? I know you're not insane. Why did you say that? He raised a good question. And I said to him brother that one must say it regardless of whether the people believe or disbelieve it was my burden. To suffer the consequences of the people's disbelief until further proof could be made known to them that the man that they all thought was dead was very much alive. I have maintained and that isn't it interesting that the 29th Surah of the Quran is called al-Ankaboot or The Spider and it says do men think that they

Farrakhan Speaks

will be left alone on saying we believe and will not be tried while others were tried before you well. That was a trial for those who walked with me. That was a trial for me. Because many of those walking with me walked timid, they didn't walk heavy. Because Farrakhan we don't know this man may have lost it. For 29 years the work of those who condemned me and Elijah has waned. And by the grace of Allah our work will continue to grow. So I will talk to you today in a way that you have never heard me before and the things that I will say to you today. Some of you will believe And some of you unfortunately will disbelieve. Some of you will come closer to me. And others will depart from me. But all of this is in the hands of Allah for the things that I

Farrakhan Speaks

say today are the things that I must say to tell
you what is coming to help to prepare you for a
world that's coming and to tell you something
about myself. I don't talk about myself. But
today I have to say something to you about me.
That The Honorable Elijah Muhammad has
already said to me time and time again, things
that I don't talk about. But today I have to say
these things and your belief or your disbelief is
not on me.

Louis Farrakhan on Power

We are Setting up a political and economic
order based on the universal principles of justice
and nd this is why both some Bibles and the
Holy Quran prophesied a Doom coming to this

Farrakhan Speaks

world for where there is no justice, there is no permanence. The Honorable Elijah Muhammad has taught us that no civilization, which is unjust whose evil outweighs its good can have any permanence in a universe constructed on the principle of justice. So when we say power at last forever, we are not speaking only of political power and economic power, but we are talking about that thing Power that makes the other two Powers permanent. That is the power that liberates the human spirit and that power my beloved brothers and sisters comes only from Allah, but when we speak of God often times we speak divisive for even though God is one. We are one are many Concepts and views of God. Speaking of politics again off times we speak

Farrakhan Speaks

divisively because we have different means on
methods of governing what we own as our
possessions. However, when we speak of me
when we speak of physical and material need
human me then we speak in Universal terms
because our physical material and human
needs. I'll pick the key the same. So this
message that we bring you this evening. We'll
focus on our common needs a common desire
to satisfy needs and the common solution that
will give us the satisfaction of all of our basic
needs. Africa the Caribbean, Black people in
America, American Indians the third world
people, people throughout the world have an
economic need. Africa has a need for the
knowledge and technology that will allow Africa

Farrakhan Speaks

to take her resources and put them into her service and the service of others. The Caribbean has that same need. Indian people in America have an economic need. Though they live on reservations they must have the knowledge and technology to transform those reservations into actual Havens for the Indian people. They need knowledge and Technology. Yes Back people in America for us. We don't have any land no mineral wealth, but what we have are the resource of the wealth and talent of our own being over which we have no Mastery. So we must regain control of ourselves. Then we must gain control of a hundred and ninety billion dollar purchasing power that we are blessed to get out of the American economy. So

Farrakhan Speaks

let us start this afternoon with Black people here in America because Black people and Indian people are a significant factor in The Liberation struggle of all oppressed people throughout the world. The Black people in America over the last four centuries of our sojourn have produced many great leaders. There are five great leaders who have left us five great Legacies. These five great leaders are Frederick Douglass, Booker T Washington, WEB Dubois, Marcus Garvey and The Honorable Elijah Muhammad Now beloved Frederick Douglass gave us the bridge And the basis for protest to demand Justice from a government and people who had deprived us of the essentials of Life Booker T. Washington gave us the A sea of black people being trained

47

Farrakhan Speaks

in agriculture and Industry that the black man
and woman May begin to do for ourselves. But
Booker T. Washington did not necessarily agree
that blacks should return to Africa, but he said
we should drop our buckets Town. Well, we are
meaning that we should draw life. From the soil
under our feet where ever we are on the earth
that is ours. Don't you ever think that the Earth
belongs to anyone but the righteous listen?
Another great legacy came from W EB your
boys. He felt that Among Us was a talented
tenth whose mind to be developed in philosophy
in the development of ideas that we should
become thinkers formulators as planners. The
Honorable Marcus Garvey wanted black people
to recognize the value of themselves and the

Farrakhan Speaks

value of Africa. He wanted blacks who were persecuted in America to return to Africa. To build Africa for the Africans at home and the world from these four great leaders and therefore great legacies come the movements that flourished in the 1960s. The civil rights movement of Martin Luther King jr. And all of the civil rights leaders Springs from the legacy of President Douglas and wev two boys a significant economic movement. However, did not spring from Booker T, Washington. Do you know why? I was so busy studying. His strategy was calling him an Uncle Tom. So when he was maligned as an Uncle Tom and those of us who came after Booker T Washington began to see him as an Uncle Tom, we didn't pay attention to

Farrakhan Speaks

what the man said. So out of Booker T,

Washington, no significant economic movement

begin. We would have produced that great

economic movement from Booker T

Washington. We wouldn't even be talking about

what we're talking about today how it lasts

forever. We would have it Marcus Garvey. Was

the father of nationalist all in America and from

mr. Garvey has thrown a significant movement

The Honorable Elijah Muhammad was similar to

these four great leaders, but yet he was

different. The Honorable Elijah Muhammad

adapted the program of nation building with the

demands of Frederick Douglass for Equal

justice. His program fulfilled The Talented tenth

concept of WEP to boy linking it with the

Farrakhan Speaks

philosophy of Booker T Washington. He asked for separation even to return to Africa or four separate states here in America. This was hard on our ears, but he also said quite simply that he could show us how to get along better with our slave masters cute. So in the germ of a seminal stage of the teachings of The Honorable Elijah Muhammad what we see is the synthesis of the approach of these four great leaders and their legacies and the basis for an entirely new civilization. So what Louis Farrakhan represents today that you consider a new Direction If Then the development of the synthesis of these four great leaders and their legacies to create from this synthesis a new movement. The national movement but a new

Farrakhan Speaks

movement that is international in scope. And this is why today you see members of the nations of Africa the Caribbean the Middle East the Indians people from all over the world represented because what we represent is not going to be bound by the geography of America. It will leave the bonus of the Atlantic Ocean and the Pacific Ocean and unite rat trap. Red and yellow people's all the way around the world and those rights of Goodwill who care to join this endeavor The Honorable Elijah Muhammad brought to black people in America our program that was religious economic education political social moral and spiritual. He dealt with the totality of our problem in the more than 40 years that he was Among Us. So you see Louis

Farrakhan Speaks

Farrakhan is developing a religious synthesis so that we can bring people of various religions and expressions together for one common cause this is why Christians are here Hebrews are here agnostics are here people have ever portrayed in a here. Why because you see Louis Farrakhan as a For your particular religious ideology. No, you see in Louis Farrakhan a man that has transcended the secularism of this kind of religious dogma and teach. Yes, but we are also developing a synthesis of the political economic and social theory of these four. That we made produce that which games and galvanized has the support of the masses of our people. Once this is done. We will have created Power to liberate ourselves on all three levels of

Farrakhan Speaks

development. What is this that we have evolved? It is called simply power. You remember how was Kwame Ture, when he was known as Stokely Carmichael said Black power and it ran white folks up a tree. Why did they get excited when the brother said power? It's because they understood that if Blacks forever achieved power Liberation is a matter of fact, you can't be liberated without power if you achieve it you liberated, but then they got us going over how to define it. I'm deeply rooted in the concept of power. When we say power. We are talking about people. Organized, listen to the words people, organized, look at the people that are here today if we were organized we got power. This is why when the brother from South

Farrakhan Speaks

Africa came here to be with us today they arrested him and arrested the top leaders. See they don't want to hear anything a Black leader in America has to say except Louis Farrakhan. Well, what is it that I'm saying that has people scared? What is it that I am saying that engenders fear in the hearts of our oppressors? Why is that I'm a very small man. I don't have much muscle mass. I'm a humble man. I've never really been in a fight in my life. Why are you so terrified at Farrakhan that you moms fight to keep me out of the college's you protect. Don't let them hear what Farrakhan has to say. What do you fear? I know what you fear. You fear the idea that I represent because of my idea from God and Mohammed. Brothers and

Farrakhan Speaks

sisters I say this with deep humility. You may not believe in my God and I may not believe in your way of representing God. But one thing we believe in we are Black people who have caught hell too long. We are Indian people who have suffered too long. We are oppressed people who have suffered.

Louis Farrakhan on Malcolm X

So I came back to America, there was no movie and I met my brother and I stood up to rebuild the work of the Honorable Elijah Muhammad. Now the movie is made and what was Warner Brothers motive. Do you mean the Jewish people who run Warner Brothers would put 30 million dollars behind a so-called anti-Semite?

Farrakhan Speaks

When somebody is Big, you know, it take a living person to get a dead man about the grave even though many of us love Malcolm. You don't have the power to raise him from the dead but white folks do and for the last six years, they've been raising Malcolm in periodicals and writings. You ain't got nothing to do with this. Its white folks orchestrating this why because six years ago or more Jesse Jackson stood up to become president. Six years ago Louis Farrakhan burst on the International scene six years ago they started battling Louis Farrakhan. And every negro they did battle they made them a booklet, but Louis Farrakhan is the only one so far who has bet his neck and God has blessed me to get stronger and stronger and

Farrakhan Speaks

stronger. So the only way they could get Farrakhan they had to raise a dead man with the purpose of using a dead man against a living black man that they have no power over. I want you to listen, this is their motive. They clean up Malcolm. They never mentioned that Malcolm was an anti-Semite. Why? They don't give a damn about Malcolm. They wanted to use Malcolm against Elijah Muhammad and push Elijah Muhammad down as the foundation upon which I stand. But their plan was even more diabolical than that. You said we going to raise Malcolm? And Spike was born to make this film but trying to get even. A little vindictiveness. He makes a movie that was brilliant. I don't think they could have got a better

Farrakhan Speaks

Malcolm. They searched the world over, Denzel took that job even the brother that played Elijah Muhammad. I don't like his script but he did a good job and even though there were negative things in the movie and yes, you know, the intent was evil, but I'm telling you brothers and sisters that movie do a lot more good than any harm, then it could do. Its what we do with what is generated from the film. Look at this two weeks after the movie came out CBS comes out with a documentary the real truth on Malcolm. Now what they're trying to do is draw me and the nation into the conflict. Because if we jump into the Controversy, then the movie would take off. They just knew we were going to jump into the fray and they were counting on that because

Farrakhan Speaks

what they really wanted to say was that Louis
Farrakhan had something to do with Malcolm's
assassination. They had it all fixed up since I
was the man that came and took Malcolm's
place in New York and came to live in the home.
that was Malcolm's and had the position that
once was Malcolm's. They could make a case
they thought saying Farrakhan was envious and
turned on Malcolm even to get Malcolm's spot
and had Malcolm bumped off. The Agents that
are working among the gangs they would be
down among you. That's why it was so
important to get the youth to the movie because
they know the youth got Vengeance in them.
They wanted to turn the guns in the community
on the Nation of Islam. And if we started fighting

Farrakhan Speaks

each other then they could bring the

government in to round up Farrakhan and the

nation of his. It was all set up and with Oprah

Winfrey and Magic Johnson and Bill Cosby

putting their money in because anything that

your money is in your concern. So if I kind of

come out beating down the movie then Oprah

would have been angry and Magic would have

been angry. They would spread it among those

people saying we have been against the middle

class and against the people that say they love

us. And Farrakhan told everybody in the nation

be quiet. I silenced the nation for 90 days. I

don't want you out in the public saying nothing

and I'm not going out in the public saying

nothing. But they wanted to raise Malcolm and

Farrakhan Speaks

kill him all over again. Wicked. They wanted to raise Malcolm and then kill him. Kill Elijah Muhammad again and above all get Farrakhan because the people are beginning to listen to him. But when I didn't say nothing, I got a stack of invitations from television from Australia from Germany from Italy. all of a sudden the movie went . Many of you were angry and one set of the brothers in the hood said I like the Malcolm that was with Elijah look like Malcolm went overseas drinking tea with them white folks and soul out. This was some of the brothers were saying then on the other hand when they were talking about Elijah he was just a dirty old man people hollering out in the theaters. Now you've got the truth. I know Malcolm shoes because I

Farrakhan Speaks

walked in them. I became the national

spokesman. On blessed Clara Muhammad's

death bed When she was at Mercy Hospital.

She asked me to come. And I visited her. I love

her like my own mother. Then tears fell from her

eyes brother Emmanuel. She said these words.

He said brother help my husband. He's getting

up in age now. Help my husband. He's not

going to let you do it. But you helped him.

Anyway, she said it ain't nothing but jealous.

Help my husband. Look at the word. Elijah

Muhammad was not jealous of me. You can't be

a jealous person or an envious person and have

the spirit of God in you. Elijah Muhammad just

tried us. And I tell you what happened to me.

People begin to praise me as the national

Farrakhan Speaks

spokesman. That Malcolm was smart. He told me before we left each other who my enemies would be. He said my enemies are going to one day be your enemies and then he said brother I wish it was you being an example for me rather than me being an example for you. As people begin to praise me, The Ministers started talking about me like a dog. And they begin to call me names. Like I was going to be the hypocrite who would lead the nation in the strain. Imagine a man working for an organization and giving it everything, God sacrificing his wife and his children and every bit of money that I had. You know, I was 42 years old and never had a bank account.

Farrakhan Speaks

Louis Farrakhan Million Man March Speech

In the name of Allah, the beneficent, the merciful. We thank Him for His prophets, and the scriptures which they brought. We thank Him for Moses and the Torah. We thank Him for Jesus and the Gospel. We thank Him for Muhammad and the Koran. Peace be upon these worthy servants of Allah. I am so grateful to Allah for His intervention in our affairs in the person of Master Farad Muhammad the Great Madi, who came among us and raised from among us a divine leader, teacher and guide, his messenger to us, the Most Honorable Elijah Muhammad. I greet all of you, my dear and wonderful brothers, with the greeting words of peace. We say it in the Arabic language, Al

Farrakhan Speaks

Salaam Alaykun. [audience responds: "Oo Alayk al salaam"]. I would like to thank all of those known and unknown persons who worked to make this day of atonement and reconciliation a reality. My thanks and my extreme gratitude to the Reverend Benjamin Chavis and to all of the members of the national organizing committees. To all of the local organizing committees, to Dr. Dorothy Height and the National Council of Negro Women, and all of the sisters who were involved in the planning of the Million Man March. Of course, if I named all those persons whom I know helped to make this event a reality, it would take a tremendous amount of time. But suffice it to say that we are grateful to all who made this day possible. We are grateful

Farrakhan Speaks

to those who put up the sound and the screens. We are grateful to all of the technical people who have made this possible. To all of the security personnel. My heartfelt thanks to Mr. Robert Johnson, the C.E.O of BET, for having the Reverend Chavis, Dr. Cornel West, and myself with Bev Smith on Our Voices to help inform our people of the purpose for the Million Man March and for taking out a full page endorsing the march in the USA Today newspaper. We thank all of the Black newspapers, radio stations, commentators, disc jockeys who really talked up the Million Man March. The mass media did not get involved until the last minute and it seemed as though they got involved with another agenda in mind.

Farrakhan Speaks

But to all of you, and we thank you the mass media too, because even though you planned it for mischief, God planned it for good. So, we thank you very much for helping to make this day successful. And to all who participated in the program and who helped to formulate the program. To all the singers, the dancers, the performers, the speakers. To all of the celebrities, to the members of the Congressional Black Caucus, to all of the religious leaders who are present, to all of the state legislators. To everyone that made this day possible, words are inadequate to express our heartfelt thanks. But really, in truth, all thanks, all praise, all honor, all glory, belongs to God. For this is the day that the Lord has made, so we are here rejoicing in

Farrakhan Speaks

this day. Certainly, to all of the members of the Nation of Islam, to all of the Ministers, Captains, Secretaries, and Sister Captains. To all of the foot soldiers who worked to raise money, that this day could be produced and hopefully all of our vendors be paid. It is not adequate to express our deep sense of personal gratitude so all I can say is thanks, thanks, thanks. Thank you. Now, where are we gathered? We're standing at the steps of the United States Capitol. I'm looking at the Washington Monument and beyond it to the Lincoln Memorial. And, beyond that, to the left, to your right, the Jefferson Memorial. Abraham Lincoln was the 16th President of these United States and he was the man who allegedly freed us.

Farrakhan Speaks

Abraham Lincoln saw in his day, what President Clinton sees in this day. He saw the great divide between Black and White. Abraham Lincoln and Bill Clinton see what the Kerner Commission saw 30 years ago when they said that this nation was moving toward two Americas—one Black, one White, separate and unequal. And the Kerner Commission revisited their findings 25 years later and saw that America was worse today than it was in the time of Martin Luther King, Jr. There's still two Americas, one Black, one White, separate and unequal. Abraham Lincoln, when he saw this great divide, he pondered a solution of separation. Abraham Lincoln said he never was in favor of our being jurors or having equal status with the Whites of

Farrakhan Speaks

this nation. Abraham Lincoln said that if there were to be a superior or inferior, he would rather the superior position be assigned to the White race. There, in the middle of this mall is the Washington Monument, 555 feet high. But if we put a 1 in front of that 555 feet, we get 1555, the year that our first fathers landed on the shores of Jamestown, Virginia as slaves. In the background is the Jefferson and Lincoln Memorial, each one of these monuments is 19 feet high. Abraham Lincoln, the sixteenth president. Thomas Jefferson, the third president, and 16 and 3 make 19 again. What is so deep about this number 19? Why are we standing on the Capitol steps today? That number 19! When you have a nine, you have a

Farrakhan Speaks

womb that is pregnant. And when you have a one standing by the nine, it means that there's something secret that has to be unfolded. Right here on this mall where we are standing, according to books written on Washington, D.C., slaves used to be brought right here on this mall in chains to be sold up and down the eastern seaboard. Right along this mall, going over to the White House, our fathers were sold into slavery. But, George Washington, the first president of the United States, said he feared that before too many years passed over his head, this slave would prove to become a most troublesome species of property. Thomas Jefferson said he trembled for this country when he reflected that God was just and that His

Farrakhan Speaks

justice could not sleep forever. Well, the day that these presidents feared has now come to pass, for on this mall, here we stand in the capital of America, and the layout of this great city, laid out by a Black man, Benjamin Banneker. This is all placed and based in a secret Masonic ritual. And at the core of the secret of that ritual is the Black man. Not far from here is the White House. And the first president of this land, George Washington, who was a grand master of the Masonic order, laid the foundation, the cornerstone of this capitol building where we stand. George was a slave owner. George was a slave owner. Now, the President spoke today and he wanted to heal the great divide. But I respectfully suggest to the

Farrakhan Speaks

President, you did not dig deep enough at the malady that divides Black and White in order to affect a solution to the problem. And so, today, we have to deal with the root so that perhaps a healing can take place. Now, this obelisk at the Washington Monument is Egyptian and this whole layout is reminiscent of our great historic past, Egypt. And, if you look at the original Seal of the United States, published by the Department of State in 1909. Gaylord Hunt wrote that late in the afternoon of July 4, 1776, the Continental Congress resolved that Dr. Benjamin Franklin, Mr. John Adams, and Mr. Thomas Jefferson be a committee to prepare a device for a Seal of the United States of America. In the design proposed by the first

Farrakhan Speaks

committee, the face of the Seal was a coat of arms measured in six quarters. That number is significant: six quarters, with emblems representing England, Scotland, Ireland, France, Germany and Holland, the countries from which the new nation had been peopled. The eye of providence in a radiant triangle and the motto, "E Pluribus Unum" were also proposed for the face of the Seal. Even though the country was populated by so-called Indians and Black slaves were brought to build the country, the official Seal of the country was never designed to reflect our presence, only that of the European immigrants. The Seal and the Constitution reflect the thinking of the founding fathers, that this was to be a nation by White

Farrakhan Speaks

people and for White people. Native Americans, Blacks, and all other non-White people were to be the burden bearers for the real citizens of this nation. For the back of the Seal, the committee suggested a picture of Pharaoh sitting in an open chariot with a crown on his head and a sword in his hand, passing through the divided waters of the Red Sea, in pursuit of the Israelites. And, hovering over the sea was to be shown a pillar of fire in a cloud, expressive of the divine presence and command. And rays from this pillar of fire were to be shown, beaming down on Moses standing on the shore, extending his hand over the sea, causing it to overwhelm Pharaoh. The motto for the reverse was "Rebellion to Tyrants is Obedience to God."

Farrakhan Speaks

Let me say it again. Rebellion to tyrants is obedience to God. Now, why did they mention Pharaoh? I heard the President say today "E Pluribus Unum"–out of many, one. But in the past, out of many comes one meant out of many Europeans come one people. The question today is, out of the many Asians, the many Arabs, the many Native Americans, the many Blacks, the many people of color who populate this country, do you mean for them to be made into the one? If so, truth has to be spoken to justice. We can't cover things up, cover them over, give it a pretty sound to make people feel good. We have to go to the root of the problem. Now, why have you come today? You came not at the call of Louis Farrakhan, but you have

Farrakhan Speaks

gathered here at the call of God. For it is only

the call of Almighty God, no matter through

whom that call came, that could generate this

kind of outpouring. God called us here to this

place, at this time, for a very specific reason.

And now, I want to say, my brothers, this is a

very pregnant moment, pregnant with the

possibility of tremendous change in our status in

America and in the world. Although the call was

made through me, many have tried to distance

the beauty of this idea from the person through

whom the idea and the call was made. Some

have done it mistakenly. And others have done

it in a malicious and vicious manner. Brothers

and sisters, there is no human being through

whom God brings an idea that history doesn't

Farrakhan Speaks

marry the idea with that human being no matter what defect was in that human being's character. You can't separate Newton from the law that Newton discovered, nor can you separate Einstein from the theory of relativity. It would be silly to try to separate Moses from the Torah or Jesus from the Gospel or Muhammad from the Koran. Well you say, "Farrakhan, you ain't no Moses, you ain't no Jesus, and you're not no Muhammad. You have a defect in your character." Well, that certainly may be so. However, according to the way the Bible reads, there is no prophet of God written of in the Bible that did not have a defect in his character. But, I have never heard any member of the faith of Judaism separate David from the Psalms,

Farrakhan Speaks

because of what happened in David's life and you never separated Solomon from the building of the Temple because they say he had a thousand concubines, and you never separated any of the Great Servants of God. So today, whether you like it or not, God brought the idea through me and he didn't bring it through me because my heart was dark with hatred and anti-Semitism, He didn't bring it through me because my heart was dark and I'm filled with hatred for White people and for the human family of the planet. If my heart were that dark, how is the message so bright, the message so clear, the response so magnificent? And so, we stand here today at this historic moment. We are standing in the place of those who could not

Farrakhan Speaks

make it here today. We are standing on the
blood of our ancestors. We are standing on the
blood of those who died in the Middle Passage,
who died in the fields and swamps of America,
who died hangin' from trees in the South, who
died in the cells of their jailers, who died on the
highways and who died in the fratricidal conflict
that rages within our community. We are
standing on the sacrifice of the lives of those
heroes, our great men and women that we
today may accept the responsibility that life
imposes upon each traveler who comes this
way. We must accept the responsibility that God
has put upon us, not only to be good husbands
and fathers and builders of our community, but
God is now calling upon the despised and the

Farrakhan Speaks

rejected to become the cornerstone and the builders of a new world. And so, our brief subject today is taken from the American Constitution. In these words, toward a more perfect union, toward a more perfect union. Now, when you use the word "more" with "perfect," that which is perfect is that which has been brought to completion. So, when you use "more perfect," you're either saying that what you call "perfect" is "perfect" for that stage of its development but not yet "complete." When Jefferson said, "toward a more perfect union," he was admitting that the union was not perfect, that it was not finished, that work had to be done. And so we are gathered here today not to bash somebody else. We're not gathered here

Farrakhan Speaks

to say all of the evils of this nation. But we are gathered here to collect ourselves for a responsibility that God is placing on our shoulders to move this nation toward a more perfect union. Now, when you look at the word "toward," "toward," it means in the direction of, in furtherance or partial fulfillment of, with the view to obtaining or having shortly before, coming soon, eminent, going on in progress. Well, that's right. We're in progress toward a perfect union. Union means bringing elements or components into unity. It is something formed by uniting two or more things. It is a number of persons, states, etcetera, which are joined or associated together for some common purpose. We're not here to tear down America. America is tearing

Farrakhan Speaks

itself down. We are here to rebuild the wasted cities. What we have in the word toward is motion. The Honorable Elijah Muhammad taught us that motion is the first law of the universe. This motion which takes us from one point to another shows that we are evolving and we are a part of a universe that is ever evolving. We are on an evolutionary course that will bring us to perfection or completion of the process toward a perfect union with God. In the word "toward" there is a law and that law is everything that is created is in harmony with the law of evolution, change. Nothing is standing still. It is either moving toward perfection or moving toward disintegration, or under certain circumstances doing both things at the same

Farrakhan Speaks

time. The word for this evolutionary changing affecting stage after stage until we reach perfection, in Arabic it is called Rhab. And from the word Rhab you get the word Rhaby, or teacher, one who nourishes a people from one stage and brings them to another stage. Well, if we are in motion, and we are, motion toward perfection and we are, there can be no motion toward perfection without the Lord, who created the law of evolution and is the master of the changes. Our first motion then must be toward the God, who created the law of the evolution of our being. And if our motion toward him is right and proper, then our motion toward a perfect union with each other and with government and with the peoples of the world will be perfected.

Farrakhan Speaks

So, let us start with a process leading to that perfect union must first be seen. Now, brothers and sisters, the day of atonement is established by God to help us achieve a closer tie with the source of wisdom, knowledge, understanding and power. For it is only through a closer union or tie with Him, who created us all, with Him who has power over all things that we can draw power, knowledge, wisdom and understanding from Him, that we may be enabled to change the realities of our life. A perfect union with God is the idea at the base of atonement. Now, atonement demands of us eight steps, in fact, atonement is the fifth step in an eight stage process. Look at our division, not here, out there. We as a people, who have been

Farrakhan Speaks

fractured, divided and destroyed, because of our division now must move toward a perfect union. Let's look at a speech delivered by a White slave holder on the banks of the James River in 1712, sixty-eight years before our former slave masters permitted us to join the Christian faith. Listen to what he said. He said, quote, "In my bag I have a fool proof method of controlling Black slaves. I guarantee everyone of you, if installed correctly, it will control the slaves for at least 300 years. My method is simple. Any member of your family or your overseer can use it. I have outlined a number of differences among the slaves and I take these differences and I make them bigger. I use fear, distrust, and envy for control purposes." I want you to listen.

Farrakhan Speaks

What are those three things? Fear, envy, distrust. For what purpose? Control. To control who? The slave. Who is the slave? Us. Listen, he said, "These methods have worked on my modest plantation in the West Indies and they will work throughout the south." "Now, take this simple little list and think about it. On the top of my list is age. But it's only there because it starts with an 'A.' And the second is color or shade. There's intelligence, sex, size of plantation, status of plantation, attitude of owners, whether the slaves live in the valley or on a hill, north, east, south or west, have fine hair or course hair, or is tall or short. Now that you have a list of differences I shall give you an outline of action. But before that, I shall assure

Farrakhan Speaks

you that distrust is stronger than trust. And envy
is stronger than adulation, respect, or
admiration. The Black slave after receiving this
indoctrination shall carry it on and will become
self-refueling and self-generating for hundreds
of years. Maybe thousands of years. Now don't
forget, you must pitch the old Black male
against the young Black male. And the young
Black male against the old Black male. You
must use the female against the male. And you
must use the male against the female. You must
use the dark skinned slave against the light
skinned slave. And the light skinned slave
against the dark skinned slave. You must also
have your white servants and overseers distrust
all Blacks. But it is necessary that your slaves

Farrakhan Speaks

trust and depend on us. They must love, respect, and trust only us. Gentlemen, these keys are your keys to control. Use them. Never miss an opportunity. And if used intensely for one year, the slaves themselves will remain perpetually distrustful. Thank you, gentlemen." End of quote. So spoke Willie Lynch 283 years ago. And so, as a consequence, we as a people now have been fractured, divided and destroyed, filled with fear, distrust and envy. Therefore, because of fear, envy and distrust of one another, many of us as leaders, teachers, educators, pastors and persons are still under the control mechanism of our former slave masters and their children. And now, in spite of all that division, in spite of all that divisiveness,

Farrakhan Speaks

we responded to a call and look at what is present here today. We have here those brothers with means and those who have no means. Those who are light and those who are dark. Those who are educated, those who are uneducated. Those who are business people, those who don't know anything about business. Those who are young, those who are old. Those who are scientific, those who know nothing of science. Those who are religious and those who are irreligious. Those who are Christian, those who are Muslim, those who are Baptist, those who are Methodist, those who are Episcopalian, those of traditional African religion. We've got them all here today. And why did we come? We came because we want to move toward a more

Farrakhan Speaks

perfect union. And if you notice, the press triggered every one of those divisions. You shouldn't come, you're a Christian. That's a Muslim thing. You shouldn't come, you're too intelligent to follow hate! You shouldn't come, look at what they did, they excluded women, you see? They played all the cards, they pulled all the strings. Oh, but you better look again, Willie. There's a new Black man in America today. A new Black woman in America today. Now brothers, there's a social benefit of our gathering here today. And that is, that from this day forward, we can never again see ourselves through the narrow eyes of the limitation of the boundaries of our own fraternal, civic, political, religious, street organization or professional

Farrakhan Speaks

organization. We are forced by the magnitude of what we see here today, that whenever you return to your cities and you see a Black man, a Black woman, don't ask him what is your social, political or religious affiliation, or what is your status? Know that he is your brother. And if he needs help, you are obligated to help your brother because he is your brother. You must live beyond the narrow restrictions of the divisions that have been imposed upon us. Well, some of us are here because it's history making. Some of us are here because it's a march through which we can express anger and rage with America for what she has and is doing to us. So, we're here for many reasons but the basic reason that this was called was for

Farrakhan Speaks

atonement and reconciliation. So, it is necessary

for me in as short of time as possible to give as

full an explanation of atonement as possible.

As I said earlier, atonement is the fifth stage in

an eight stage process. So, let's go back to the

first stage of the process that brings us into

perfect union with God. And the first stage is the

most difficult of all because when we are wrong,

and we are not aware of it, someone has to

point out the wrong. I want to, I want to say this

again, but I want to say it slowly. And I really

want each one of these points to sink in. How

many of us in this audience, at some time or

another have been wrong? Would we just raise

our hands? OK. Now, when we are wrong, Lord

knows we want to be right. The most difficult

Farrakhan Speaks

thing is when somebody points it out do we accept it, do we reject it, do we hate the person who pointed out our wrong? How do we treat the person who points out our wrong? Now, I want you to follow me. When you go to a doctor, you're not feeling well, the doctor says, what's wrong? Well, I don't know, doc. Well, where is the pain? Tell me something about the symptoms. You want the doctor to make a correct diagnosis. You don't smack the doctor when he points out what's wrong. You don't hate the doctor when he points out what's wrong. You say, thank you, doctor. What's my prescription for healing? We all right? [audience responds: "Yeah"]. Now, look, whoever is entrusted with the task of pointing out wrong,

Farrakhan Speaks

depending on the nature of the circumstances,
is not always loved. In fact, more than likely, that
person is going to be hated and misunderstood.
Such persons are generally hated because no
one wants to be shown as being wrong.
Particularly when you're dealing with
governments, with principalities, with powers,
with rulers, with administrations. When you're
dealing with forces which have become
entrenched in their evil, intractable and
unyielding their power produces an arrogance.
And their arrogance produces a blindness. And
out of that evil state of mind, they will do all
manner of evil to the person who points out their
wrong. Even though you're doing good for them
by pointing out where America went wrong.

Farrakhan Speaks

Now, Martin Luther King, Jr. was probably one of the most patriotic Americans. More patriotic than George Washington. More patriotic than Thomas Jefferson. More patriotic than many of the presidents because he had the courage to point out what was wrong in the society. And because he pointed out what was wrong, he was evil spoken of, vilified, maligned, hated and eventually, murdered. Brother Malcolm had that same road to travel. He pointed out what was wrong in the society and he had to suffer for pointing out what was wrong and he ultimately died on the altar for pointing out what was wrong. Inside the nation, outside the nation, to the greater nation and to the smaller nation.

Farrakhan Speaks

We talking about moving toward a perfect union. Well, pointing out fault, pointing out our wrongs is the first step. The second step is to acknowledge. Oh, thank you. Oh, man, I'm wrong. To acknowledge means to admit the existence, the reality or the truth of some reality. It is to recognize as being valid. Or having force and power. It is to express thanks, appreciation, or gratitude. So in this context, the word acknowledgement means to be in a state of recognition of the truth of the fact that we have been wrong. This is the second step. Well, the third step is that after you know you're wrong and you acknowledge it to yourself, who else knows it except you confess it. You say, well, yeah, all right. But who should I confess to?

Farrakhan Speaks

And why should I confess? The Bible says confession is good for the soul. Now, brothers I know, I don't have a lot of time, but the soul is the essence of a person's being. And when the soul is covered with guilt from sin and wrongdoing, the mind and the actions of the person reflect the condition of the soul. So, to free the soul or the essence of man from its burden, one must acknowledge one's wrong, but then one must confess. The Holy Koran says it like this: I've been greatly unjust to myself, and I confess my faults. So grant me protection against all my faults, for none grants protection against faults but Thee. It is only through confession that we can be granted protection from the consequences of our faults.

Farrakhan Speaks

For every deed has a consequence. And we can never be granted protection against the faults that we refuse to acknowledge or that we are unwilling to confess. So, look. Who should you confess to? I don't want to confess. Who should you confess to? Who should I confess to? Who should we confess to? First, you confess to God. And everyone of us that are here today, that knows that we have done wrong, we have to go to God and speak to Him in the privacy of our rooms and confess. He already knows, but when you confess, you're relieving your soul of the burden that it bears. But, then, the hardest part is to go to the person or persons whom your fault has ill-affected and confess to them. That's hard. That's hard. But, if we want a

Farrakhan Speaks

perfect union, we have to confess the fault.

Well, what happens after confession? There

must be repentance. When you repent, you feel

remorse or contrition or shame for the past

conduct which was and is wrong and sinful. It

means to feel contrition or self-reproach for what

one has done or failed to do. And, it is the

experiencing of such regret for past conduct that

involves the changing of our mind toward that

sin. So, until we repent and feel sick, sorry over

what we have done, we can never, never,

change our mind toward that thing. And if you

don't repent, you'll do it over and over and over

again. But to stop it where it is, and Black men,

we got to stop what we're doing where it is. We

cannot continue the destruction of our lives and

Farrakhan Speaks

the destruction of our community. But that change can't come until we feel sorry. I heard my brother from the West Coast say today, I atone to the mothers for the death of the babies caused by our senseless slaughter of one another. See, when he feels sorry deep down inside, he's going to make a change. That man has a change in his mind. That man has a change in his heart. His soul has been unburdened and released from the pain of that sin, but you got to go one step further, because after you've acknowledged it, confessed it, repented, you've come to the fifth stage. Now you've got to do something about it. Now, look brothers, sisters. Some people don't mind confessing. Some people don't mind making

Farrakhan Speaks

some slight repentance. But, when it comes to doing something about the evil that we've done, we fall short. But atonement means satisfaction or reparation for a wrong or injury. It means to make amends. It means penance, expiation, compensation and recompense made or done for an injury or wrong. So, atonement means we must be willing to do something in expiation of our sins so we can't just have a good time today, and say we made history in Washington. We got to resolve today that we're going back home to do something about what's going on in our lives and in our families and in our communities. Now, we all right? Can you hang with me a few more? Now, brothers and sisters, if we make atonement it leads to the sixth stage.

Farrakhan Speaks

And the sixth stage is forgiveness. Now, so many of us want forgiveness, but we don't want to go through the process that leads to it. And so, when we say we forgive, we forgive from our lips, but we have never pardoned in the heart. So, the injury still remains. My dear family. My dear brothers. We need forgiveness. God is always ready to forgive us for our failures. Forgiveness means to grant pardon for, or remission of, an offense or sin. It is to absolve, to clear, to exonerate and to liberate. Boy, that's something! See, you're not liberated until you can forgive. You're not liberated from the evil effect of our own sin until we can ask God for forgiveness and then forgive others, and this is why in the Lord's Prayer you say, forgive us our

Farrakhan Speaks

trespasses as we forgive those who trespass against us. So, it means to cease to feel offense and resentment against another for the harm done by an offender. It means to wipe the slate clean. And then, that leads to the seventh stage. You know, I like to liken this to music. Because in music, the seventh note is called a leading tone. [Farrakhan sings] Do, Re, Mi, Fa, So, La, Ti. You can't stop there. Ti. It leaves you hung up, Ti. What you got to get back to? Do. So, whatever you started with when you reach the eight note, you're back to where you started only at a higher vibration. Now, look, at this. The seventh tone, the leading tone that leads to the perfect union with God is reconciliation and restoration because after forgiveness, now, we

Farrakhan Speaks

are going to be restored to what? To our original position. To restore, to reconcile means to become friendly, peaceable again, to put hostile persons into a state of agreement or harmony, to make compatible or to compose or settle what it was that made for division. It means to resolve differences. It can mean to establish or re-establish a close relationship between previously hostile persons. So, restoration means the act of returning something to an original or un-impaired condition. Now, when you're back to an un-impaired position, you have reached the eighth stage, which is perfect union. And when we go through all these steps, there is no difference between us, that we can't heal. There's a bomb in Gilead to heal the sin

Farrakhan Speaks

sick soul. There is a bomb in Gilead to make the wounded whole. We are a wounded people but we're being healed, but President Clinton, America is also wounded. And there's hostility now in the great divide between the people. Socially the fabric of America is being torn apart and it's Black against Black, Black against White, White against White, White against Black, Yellow against Brown, Brown against Yellow. We are being torn apart. And we can't gloss it over with nice speeches, my dear, Mr. President. Sir, with all due respect, that was a great speech you made today. And you praised the marchers and they're worthy of praise. You honored the marchers and they are worthy of honor. But of course, you spoke ill indirectly of

Farrakhan Speaks

me, as a purveyor of malice and hatred. I must

hasten to tell you, Mr. President, that I'm not a

malicious person, and I'm not filled with malice.

But, I must tell you that I come in the tradition of

the doctor who has to point out, with truth,

what's wrong. And the pain is that power has

made America arrogant. Power and wealth has

made America spiritually blind and the power

and the arrogance of America makes you refuse

to hear a child of your slaves pointing out the

wrong in your society. But, I think if you could

clear the scales from your eyes, sir, and give

ear to what we say, perhaps, oh perhaps, what

these great speakers who spoke before me

said, and my great and wonderful brother, the

Reverend Jesse Jackson said, and perhaps,

Farrakhan Speaks

just perhaps, from the children of slaves might
come a solution to this Pharaoh and this Egypt
as it was with Joseph when they had to get him
out of prison and wash him up and clean him up
because Pharaoh had some troubling dreams
that he didn't have any answer to. He called his
soothsayers and he called the people that read
the stars and he called all his advisors, but
nobody could help him to solve the problem. But
he had to go to the children of slaves, because
he heard that there was one in prison who knew
the interpretation of dreams. And he said bring
him, bring him and let me hear what he has to
say. God has put it for you in the scriptures, Mr.
President. Balshasar and Nebuchadnezzar
couldn't read the handwriting on the wall. But,

Farrakhan Speaks

Daniel had to read the handwriting for him. Your kingdom has been weighed in the balance and has been found wanting. Do you want a solution to the dilemma that America faces? Then, don't look at our skin color, because racism will cause you to reject salvation if it comes in the skin of a Black person. Don't look at the kinkiness of our hair and the broadness of our nose and the thickness of our lips, but listen to the beat of our hearts and the pulsating rhythm of the truth. Perhaps, perhaps, you might be as wise as that Pharaoh and save this great nation. And so, the eighth stage is perfect union with God. And in the Koran, it reads. "Oh soul that is at rest, well pleased with thy lord and well pleasing." Oh, brothers, brothers, brothers, you don't know

Farrakhan Speaks

what its like to be free. Freedom can't come from White folks. Freedom can't come from staying here and petitioning this great government. We're here to make a statement to the great government, but not to beg them. Freedom cannot come from no one but the god who can liberate the soul from the burden of sin. And this is why Jesus said "come unto me," not some who are heavy laden, "but all that are heavy laden, and I will give you rest. But listen, all of these eight steps take place in a process called time. And whenever a nation is involved in sin to the point that God intends to judge and destroy that nation, he always sends someone to make that nation or people know their sins, to reflect on it, to acknowledge, to confess, to

Farrakhan Speaks

repent and to atone that they might find forgiveness with God. America, oh America. This great city of Washington is like Jerusalem. And the Bible says "Jerusalem, oh Jerusalem, you that stoneth and killith the prophets of God." Right from this beautiful Capitol and from the beautiful White House have come commands to kill the prophets. Garvey's trouble came from this house. Martin Luther King's trouble came from this house. Malcolm's trouble came from this house. W. E. B. Dubois' trouble came from this house. And from this house, you stoned and killed the prophets of God that would have liberated Black people, liberated America. But I stand here today knowing, knowing that you are angry. That my people have validated me. I

Farrakhan Speaks

don't need you to validate me. I don't need to be in any mainstream. I want to wash in the river of Jordan and the river that you see and the sea that is before us and behind us and around us is validation. That's the mainstream. You're out of touch with reality. A few of you in a few smoke-filled rooms, calling that the mainstream while the masses of the people, White and Black, Red, Yellow, and Brown, poor and vulnerable are suffering in this nation. Well, America, great America. Like Jerusalem that stoned and killed the prophets of God. That a work has been done in you today unlike any work that's ever been done in this great city. I wonder what you'll say tomorrow? I wonder what you'll write in your newspapers and magazines, tomorrow. Will you

113

Farrakhan Speaks

give God the glory? Will you give God the glory? Will you respect the beauty of this day? All of these Black men that the world sees as savage, maniacal, and bestial. Look at them. A sea of peace. A sea of tranquility. A sea of men ready to come back to God. Settle their differences and go back home to turn our communities into decent and safe places to live. America. America, the beautiful. There's no country like this on the earth. And certainly if I lived in another country, I might never have had the opportunity to speak as I speak today. I probably would have been shot outright and so would my brother, Jesse, and so would Maulana Karenga and so would Dr. Ben Chavis and Reverend Al Sampson and all the wonderful

Farrakhan Speaks

people that are here. But because this is
America you allow me to speak even though
you don't like what I may say. Because this is
America, that provision in the constitution for
freedom of speech and freedom of assembly
and freedom of religion, that is your saving
grace. Because what you're under right now is
grace. And grace is the expression of divine
love and protection which God bestows freely
on people. God is angry, America. He's angry,
but His mercy is still present. Brothers and
sisters look at the inflictions that have come
upon us in the Black community. Do you know
why we're being afflicted? God wants us to
humble ourselves to the message that will make
us atone and come back to Him and make

Farrakhan Speaks

ourselves whole again. But why is God afflicting America? Why is God afflicting the world? Why did Jesus say there would be wars and rumors of wars, and earthquakes in diverse places and pestilence and famine, and why did He say that these were just the beginning of sorrows? In the last ten years America has experienced more calamities than at any other time period in American history. Why America? God is angry. He's not angry because you're right. He's angry because you're wrong and you want to stone and kill the people who want to make you see you're wrong. And so, the Bible says Elijah must first come. Why should Elijah come? Elijah has the job of turning the hearts of the children back to their fathers, and the father's heart back to

Farrakhan Speaks

the children. Elijah becomes an axis upon which people turn back to God and God turns back to the people. And that's why it said Elijah must first come. And so, here we are, 400 years, fulfilling Abraham's prophecy. Some of our friends in the religious community have said, why should you take atonement? That was for the children of Israel. I say yes, it was. But atonement for the children of Israel prefigured our suffering here in America. Israel was in bondage to Pharaoh 400 years. We've been in America 440 years. They were under affliction. We're under affliction. They're under oppression. We're under oppression. God said that nation which they shall serve, I will judge. Judgment means God is making a decision

Farrakhan Speaks

against systems, against institutions, against principalities and powers. And that's why Paul said, we war not against flesh and blood, but against principalities and powers, and the rulers of the darkness of this world and spiritual wickedness in high places. God is sending His decision. I can't help it if I've got to make the decision known. You don't understand me. My people love me. And yet, and yet, I point out the evils of Black people like no other leader does, but my people don't call me anti-Black, because they know I must love them in order to point out what's wrong so we can get it right to come back into the favor of God! But, let me say in truth, you can't point out wrong with malice. You can't point out wrong with hatred. Because, if we

Farrakhan Speaks

point out wrong with bitterness and hatred, then

the bitterness and the hatred becomes a barrier

between you and the person whom you hope to

get right that they might come into the favor of

God. So, we as Muslims who, in our first stage,

yeah, we pointed out the wrong of America, but

we didn't point it out with no love, we point it out

with the pain of our hurt. The pain of our

suffering. The bitterness of our life story. But, we

have grown beyond our bitterness. We have

transcended beyond our pain. Why? It's easy for

us to say, the White man did this, the White man

did that, the White man did the other, the White

man did this. He deprived us of that. He killed

the Indians. He did this. Yes, he did all of that.

But, why did God let him do that? That's the

Farrakhan Speaks

bigger question. And since we are not man enough to question God, we start beating up on the agent who is fulfilling prophesy. But, if we can transcend our pain to get up into God's mind, and ask God, "God, why did you let our fathers come into bondage? God, why did you let us die in the Middle Passage? God, why did you suffer us to be in the hulls of ships? God, why did you let him lash us, why did you let him beat us, why did you let him castrate us? Why did you let him hang us? Why did you let him burn us? Why, God, why, why, why?" We got a right to question God. That's the only way we can become wise. And if we question him like Job did, God may bring you up into his own thinking. And if God were to answer us today he

Farrakhan Speaks

would say to Black people, yes, I allowed this to happen. And I know you suffered, but Martin King, my servant, said it, undeserved suffering is redemptive. A whole world is lost, not just you Black people. A whole world has gone out of the way, not just you Black people. You the lost sheep, but the whole world is lost. You the bottom rail, but the one that put you on the bottom is then in the bottom with you holding you down. He's in the bottomless pit himself. He said, Black Man, I love you. He said, but God, I mean, that's a heck of a way to show me you love me. He said, but I love my son. I love Jesus more than I love any of my servants. But I had a cross for him. I had nails for him. I had him to be rejected and despised. I had him

Farrakhan Speaks

falsely accused and brought before the courts of men. I had them spit on him. I had them to pierce his side. But, I loved him more than anybody else. Why, God?! Why did you do it? Why? He said, I did it that I might be glorified, because like Job, no matter what I did to him, he never cursed me, he never said my God ain't no good. He said whatever your will is, that's what I want to do and that's why, even though he descended into Hell, I have raised him to the limitless heights of Heaven, because only those who know the depths of Hell can appreciate the limitless heights of Heaven. And so, my children, I caused you to suffer in the furnace of affliction so that I might purify you and resurrect you from a grave of death and ignorance. I,

Farrakhan Speaks

God, put in your soul, not a law written on stone, but I have written the law on the tablets of your heart. So, I'm going to make a new covenant with you. Oh, Black man. The eagles are gathered together, there shall the carcass be. Here's the carcass, the remains of a once mighty people, dry bones in the valley, a people slain from the foundation of the world. But God has sent the winds to blow on the bones. One of those winds is named Gingrich. And the companion wind is named Dole. And the other is called Supreme Court decision. The other is fratricidal conflict, drugs and dope and violence and crime. But we've had enough now. This is why you're in Washington today. We've had enough. We've had enough distress, enough

Farrakhan Speaks

affliction. We're ready to bow down now. If my people, who are called by my name, would just humble themselves and pray, and seek my face, and turn from their wicked ways, then will I hear from heaven, forgive their sins, heal their land. You are ready now to come out of your furnace of affliction. You are ready now to accept the responsibility, oh, not just of the ghetto. God wants to purify you and lift you up, that you may call America and the world to repentance. Black man, you are a master builder, but you got hit in the head. Black men, you're the descendants of the builders of the pyramids. But you have amnesia now. You can't remember how you did it. But the Master has come. You know, pastors, I love that scripture where Jesus told his

Farrakhan Speaks

disciples, go there and you'll see an ass and a colt tied with her. Untie 'em and bring 'em to me. If anybody ask you what you're doing, because it may look like you're stealing and you know they love to accuse you of stealing, tell them the Master got need of these. And Jesus rode into Jerusalem on an ass. The Democratic Party has for its symbol, a donkey. The donkey stands for the unlearned masses of the people. But the Democratic Party can't call them asses no more. You got 'em all tied up, but you're not using 'em. The donkey is tied up. But can you get off today? No, I can't get off, I'm tied up. Somebody on you donkey? Well, yeah. I got a master. He rides me like the Master rode Balem's ass, you know. But, hell, the ass is now talking with a

Farrakhan Speaks

man's voice. And the ass want ta throw the rider off, because he got a new rider today. If anybody ask you, tell them the Master has need. Look at you. Oh, I don't know what the number is. It's too much for me to count. But I think they said it's a million and a half, or two. I don't know how many. But you know, I called for a million. When I saw the word go out my mouth, I looked at it. I said, "Oh my God!" It just came out of my mouth. I didn't know. And after it came out, I said, "Well I got to go with it." And, I'm so glad I did. People told me you better change that figure to one more realistic. And I should have changed it to the Three Million Man March. Now, we're almost finished. I want to take one last look at the word "atonement." The

Farrakhan Speaks

first four letters of the word form the foundation: "a-t-o-n" . . . "a-ton," "a-ton." Since this obelisk in front of us is representative of Egypt. In the 18th dynasty, a Pharaoh named Akhenaton, was the first man of this history period to destroy the pantheon of many gods and bring the people to the worship of one god. And that one god was symbolized by a sun disk with 19 rays coming out of that sun with hands holding the Egyptian Ankh–the cross of life. A-ton. The name for the one god in ancient Egypt. A- ton, the one god. 19 rays. Look at your scripture. A woman, remember the nine means somebody pregnant, with an idea. But, in this case, it's a woman pregnant with a male child destined to rule the nations with a rod of iron. God is standing over

Farrakhan Speaks

her womb, and this child will be like the day sun, and He will say "I am the light of the world." Hands coming out of that sun, come unto me all ye that are heavy laden. I'm going to give you rest, but I'm going to give you life, because I am the resurrection and the life and if you believe in me, though you are dead, yet shall you live again. You're dead, Black man. But if you believe in the god who created this sun of truth and of light with 19 rays, meaning he's pregnant with God's spirit, God's life, God's wisdom. Abraham Lincoln's statue, 19 feet high, 19 feet wide. Jefferson, 19 feet high, 16, and the third president, 19. Standing on the steps of the Capitol, in the light of the sun. Offering life to a people who are dead. Black man, the a-ton

Farrakhan Speaks

represents the one God. In the Koran,

Muhammad is called a light giving son. So if you

look at the a-ton, add an "e" to it, and separate

the "a" from the next four letters and you get the

word atone. "Tone" means sound. And "a", the

first letter of the alphabet and the first letter of

the numerical system is one. So "a" equals one.

So "a" sound means when you hear the "a"

tone, you will hear the right sound. And when

you hear the right sound from the one God

calling you to divine life, you will respond. So

what is the "a" tone? In music, "a" equals 440

vibrations. How long have we been in America?

Four hundred and forty years. Well, in the 440th

year, from the one God, the aton will come the

"a" tone and all of us got to tune up our lives by

Farrakhan Speaks

the sound of the a tone. Because we've got to
atone for all that we have done wrong. And
when you atone, if you take the "t" and couple it
with the "a" and hyphenate it, you get "at-one."
So when you atone you become at one. At one
with who? The aton or the one God. Because
you heard the "a" tone and you tuned up your
life and now you're ready to make a new
beginning. So when you get at one, you get the
next two letters. It is "m" "e." Me. Who is it that
has to atone? [audience responds: "Me"] Who?
["Me"] Who went wrong? ["Me"] Who got to fix
it? ["Me"] Who should we look to? ["Me"] Yes!
And then if you add, if you add another letter to
"me" you get an "n." What does that say?
["Men"] Men. So Farrakhan called men. Why did

Farrakhan Speaks

you call men? Because in the beginning, God made man. And if we are at a new beginning, we got to make a man all over again, but make him in the image and the likeness of God. Now, if you add the "t" on, you get the suffix "ment." Ment means action, process. The instrument or agent of an action or process. So when you say I'm atoning, you got to act on it. You gotta get in the process. You gotta acknowledge your wrong, confess your wrong. Repent of your wrong. Atone for your wrong. Huh? Then you'll get forgiveness, then reconciliation, and restoration. And then you're back to the atone. Oh, Lord. Now brothers, let's close it out. Don't move. Don't move. Now you know the Bible says in the 430th year of this sojourn they went

Farrakhan Speaks

out. That's in a book called Exodus. Now the
word exodus means departure–a going out. A
way out. What did we come to Washington for?
We didn't come to Washington to petition the
government for a way out of her. But to find a
way out of our affliction. But a way out from
something bigger than our affliction. Oh, man.
When you say come out, what do you mean?
You've got to come out from under the mind of a
slave. We've got to come out from a mind that is
self-afflicted with the evil of Black inferiority.
We've got to come into a new way of thinking.
Now brothers, sisters, I want to close this lecture
with a special message to our President and to
the Congress. There is a great divide, but the
real evil in America is not white flesh, or black

Farrakhan Speaks

flesh. The real evil in America is the idea that undergirds the set up of the western world. And that idea is called White supremacy. Now wait, wait, wait. Before you get angry. Those of you listening by television. You don't even know why you behave the way you behave. I'm not telling you I'm a psychiatrist, but I do want to operate on your head. White supremacy is the enemy of both White people and Black people because the idea of White supremacy means you should rule because you're White, that makes you sick. And you've produced a sick society and a sick world. The founding fathers meant well, but they said, "toward a more perfect union." So, the Bible says, we know in part, we prophesy in part, but when that which is perfect is come, that

Farrakhan Speaks

which is in part shall be done away with. So either, Mr. Clinton, we're going to do away with the mind-set of the founding fathers. You don't have to repudiate them like you've asked my brothers to do me. You don't have to say they were malicious, hate filled people. But you must evolve out of their mind-set. You see their mind was limited to those six European nations out of which this country was founded. But you've got Asians here. How are you going to handle that? You've got children of Africa here. How are you going to handle that? You've got Arabs here. You've got Hispanics here. I know you call them illegal aliens, but hell, you took Texas from them by flooding Texas with people that got your mind. And now they're coming back across the

Farrakhan Speaks

border to what is Northern Mexico, Texas, Arizona, New Mexico, and California. They don't see themselves as illegal aliens. I think they might see you as an illegal alien. You have to be careful how you talk to people. You have to be careful how you deal with people. The Native American is suffering today. He's suffering almost complete extinction. Now, he learned about bingo. You taught him. He learned about black jack. You taught him. He learned about playing roulette. You taught him. Now, he's making a lot of money. You're upset with him because he's adopted your ways. What makes you like this? See, you're like this because you're not well. You're not well. And in the light of today's global village, you can never

Farrakhan Speaks

harmonize with the Asians. You can't harmonize
with the islands of the Pacific. You can't
harmonize with the dark people of the world who
outnumber you eleven to one, if you're going to
stay in the mind of White supremacy. White
supremacy has to die in order for humanity to
live. Now, oh, I know. I know. I know it's painful,
but we have to operate now, just, just take a
little of this morphine and you won't feel the pain
as much. You just need to bite down on
something, as I stop this last few minutes, just
bite down on your finger. Listen, listen, listen,
listen, White supremacy caused you all, not you
all, some White folk to try to rewrite history and
write us out. White supremacy caused Napoleon
to blow the nose off of the Sphinx because it

Farrakhan Speaks

reminded you too much of the Black man's

majesty. White supremacy caused you to take

Jesus, a man with hair like lambs wool and feet

like burnished brass and make him White. So

that you could worship him because you could

never see yourself honoring somebody Black

because of the state of your mind. You see, you,

you really need help. You'll be all right. You'll be

all right. You will be all right. Now, now, now,

you painted the Last Supper, everybody there

White. My mother asked the man that came to

bring her the Bible. He said, look there, the

pictures in the Bible. You see, Jesus and all his

disciples are at the Last Supper—my mother in

her West Indian accent said, you mean ain't

nobody Black was at the Last Supper? And the

Farrakhan Speaks

man said, "Yes, but they was in the kitchen." So now you've whitened up everything. Any great invention that we made you put White on it, because you didn't want to admit that a Black person had that intelligence, that genius. You try to color everything to make it satisfactory to the sickness of your mind. So you whitened up religion, Farrakhan didn't do that. You locked the Bible from us, Farrakhan didn't do that. Your sick mind wouldn't even let you bury us in the same ground that both of us came out of. We had to be buried somewhere else. That's sick. Some of us died just to drink water out of a fountain marked White. That's sick. Isn't it sick? You poisoned religion. And in all the churches, until recently, the master was painted white. So,

Farrakhan Speaks

you had us bowing down to your image. Which

ill-effected our minds. You gave us your version

of history. And you whitened that up. Yes, you

did. Yes, you did. You are a White Shriner. The

Black Shriner don't integrate the shrine. Why

don't you Black Shriners integrate the shrine?

Because in the shrine, you are the essence of

the secret. They don't want you there. They'll

have to tell the world, it's you we been thinking

about all along. Now, White folks see the reason

you could look at the O.J. Simpson trial, in

horror, and the reason Black folk rejoiced, had

nothing to do with the horror of the tragedy.

Black folk would never rejoice over the slaughter

of Ron Goldman and Nicole Brown Simpson.

Black folk saw that with compassion. Many

Farrakhan Speaks

Black folk grieve over that reality. You say, "O.J. sold out." No, he didn't sell out. He was drawn out. Black folk that got talent, they all grow up in the "hood." When we first sing, we sing in these old raunchy night clubs in the "hood." When we play sandlot ball, we play it in the "hood." But when you spot us, you draw us out. You say "that Negro can run. Look at how high he jumps." So you give us a scholarship to your university. But the Blacks who are in college, who play basketball for you, who play football for you, who run track for you, you disallow them to get involved with Black students and the suffering of Black students on all-White campuses. You hide them away. Give them privileges. Then they find themselves with your

Farrakhan Speaks

daughter. Then you take them into the NBA, the NFL, and they become megastars. Or in the entertainment field and when they become megastars, their association is no longer Black. They may not have a Black manager, a Black agent, a Black accountant. They meet in parties, in posh neighborhoods that Black folk don't come into. So their association becomes White women, White men, and association breeds assimilation. And if you have a slave mentality, you feel you have arrived now because you can jump over cars, running in airports, playing in films. I'm not degrading, my brother, I love him. But he was drawn out. He didn't sell out, he was drawn out. Michael Jackson is drawn out. Most of our top stars are drawn out. And then, when

Farrakhan Speaks

you get them, you imprison them with fear and distrust. You don't want them to speak out on the issues that are political, that are social. They must shut their mouths or you threaten to take away their fame, take away their fortune because you're sick. And the president is not gonna point this out. He's trying to get well. But he's a physician that can't heal himself. I'm almost finished. White supremacy has poisoned the bloodstream of religion, education, politics, jurisprudence, economics, social ethics and morality. And there is no way that we can integrate into White supremacy and hold our dignity as human beings because if we integrate into that, we become subservient to that. And to become subservient to that is to make the slave

Farrakhan Speaks

master comfortable with his slave. So, we got to come out of here my people. Come out of a system and a world that is built on the wrong idea. An idea that never can create a perfect union with God. The false idea of White supremacy prevents anyone from becoming one with God. White people have to come out of that idea, which has poisoned them into a false attitude of superiority based on the color of their skins. The doctrine of White supremacy disallows Whites to grow to their full potential. It forces White people to see themselves as the law or above the law. And that's why Furhman could say that he is like a god. See, he thinks like that, but that idea is pervasive in police departments across the country. And it's getting

Farrakhan Speaks

worse and not better because White supremacy is not being challenged. And I say to all of us who are leaders, all of us who are preachers, we must not shrink from the responsibility of pointing out wrong, so that we can be comfortable and keep White people comfortable in their alienation from God. And so, White folks are having heart attacks today because their world is coming down. And if you look at the Asians, the Asians have the fastest growing economies in the world. The Asians are not saying, bashing White people. You don't find the Asians saying the White man is this, the White man is that, the White man is the other. He don't talk like that. You know what he does? He just relocates the top banks from Wall Street to

Farrakhan Speaks

Tokyo. He don't say, "I'm better than the White man." He just starts building his world and building his economy and challenging White supremacy. I saw a young 14-year-old Chinese girl the other day play the violin. Sarah Chang is her name. She was magnificent. I saw a young Japanese girl, Midori, play the violin. She was magnificent. They don't have to say to White people, "I'm better than you." They just do their thing. And White folk have to readjust their thinking, because they thought that they could master all of these instruments and nobody else could, but the Chinese are mastering it, the Japanese are mastering it. All these things are breaking up the mind of White supremacy. Black man, you don't have to bash White people, all

145

Farrakhan Speaks

we got to do is go back home and turn our communities into productive places. All we gotta do is go back home and make our communities a decent and safe place to live. And if we start dotting the Black community with businesses, opening up factories, challenging ourselves to be better than we are, White folk, instead of driving by, using the "N" word, they'll say, "Look, look at them. Oh, my God. They're marvelous. They're wonderful. We can't, we can't say they're inferior anymore." But, every time we drive-by shoot, every time we carjack, every time we use foul, filthy language, every time we produce culturally degenerate films and tapes, putting a string in our women's backside and parading them before the world, every time we

Farrakhan Speaks

do things like this we are feeding the

degenerate mind of White supremacy and I

want us to stop feeding that mind and let that

mind die a natural death. And so, to all the

artists that are present, you wonderful gifted

artists, remember that your gift comes from

God. And David the Psalmist said, "praise Him

on the tumbrel, praise Him on the lute, praise

Him on the harp, praise Him in the sultry, praise

Him in the song, praise Him in the dance, let

everything be a praise of God." So, when you

sing, you don't have to get naked to sing.

Demonstrate your gift, not your breast.

Demonstrate your gift, not what is between your

legs. Clean up, Black man, and the world will

respect and honor you. But, you have fallen

Farrakhan Speaks

down like the prodigal son and you're husking corn and feeding swine. Filthy jokes. We can't bring our children to the television. We can't bring our families to the movies because the American people have an appetite like a swine. And you are feeding the swine with the filth of degenerate culture. We got to stop it. We're not putting you down, brothers, we want to pick you up so with your rap, you can pick up the world. With your song, you can pick up the world. With your dance, with your music, you can pick up the world. And so America, if your conscience is afflicted because God is lashing you, don't just start with the constitution, Mr. President. Start with the evil of slavery because that's the root of the problem. And you can't solve the problem,

Farrakhan Speaks

Mr. President, unless we expose the root. For when you expose the root to the light, then the root will die. The tree will die. And something new can come to birth. And so to the Whites of this nation, except you be born again, you can not see the kingdom of God. But can I return back into my mother's womb for the second time? No. You can't do that. But this old mind of White supremacy has to die in order that a new mind might come to birth. Black man. You can't see the kingdom of God unless we be born again. Must I enter back into my mother's womb for a second time? No. You can't do that Black man. But the mind of White supremacy is repulsive to God. And the mind of Black inferiority is repulsive to God. And any mind of

Farrakhan Speaks

Black supremacy is repulsive to God. But the
only mind that God will accept is a mind stayed
on him and on righteousness. Black had to be
taught to give us root in loving ourselves again.
But that was a medicine, a prescription. But
after health is restored we can't keep taking the
medicine. We've got to move onto something
else. Higher and better. So, my beloved
brothers and sisters, here's what we would like
you to do. Everyone of you, my dear brothers,
when you go home, here's what I want you to
do. We must belong to some organization that is
working for and in the interest of the uplift and
the liberation of our people. Go back, join the
NAACP if you want to, join the Urban league,
join the All African People's Revolutionary Party,

Farrakhan Speaks

join us, join the Nation of Islam, join PUSH, join
the Congress of Racial Equality, join SCLC, the
Southern Christian Leadership Conference, but
we must become a totally organized people and
the only way we can do that is to become a part
of some organization that is working for the uplift
of our people. We must keep the local
organizing committees that made this event
possible, we must keep them together. Go back
and join the local organizing committee. And
then all of us, as leaders, must stay together
and make the National African American
Leadership Summit inclusive of all of us. I know
that the NAACP did not officially endorse this
march. Neither did the Urban League. But, so
what? So what? Many of the members are here

Farrakhan Speaks

anyway. I know that Dr. Lyons, of the National Baptist Association USA did not endorse the march, nor did the Reverend Dr. B.W. Smith, nor did Bishop Chandler Owens, but so what? These are our brothers and we're not going to stop reaching out for them simply because we feel there was a misunderstanding. We still want to talk to our brothers because we cannot let artificial barriers divide us. Remember the letter of Willie Lynch and let's not let Willie Lynch lynch our new spirit and our new attitude and our new mind. No, we must continue to reach out for those that have condemned this, and make them to see that this was not evil: it was not intended for evil, it was intended for good. Now, brothers, moral and spiritual renewal is a

Farrakhan Speaks

necessity. Every one of you must go back home and join some church, synagogue, temple or mosque that is teaching spiritual and moral uplift. I want you, brothers, there's no men in the church, in the mosque. The men are in the streets and we got to get back to the houses of God. But preachers, we have to revive religion in America. We have to revive the houses of God that they're not personal thiefdoms of those of us who are their preachers and pastors. But we got to be more like Jesus, more like Mohammed, more like Moses and become servants of the people in fulfilling their needs. Brothers, when you go home, we've got to register eight million, eligible but unregistered brothers, sisters. So you go home and find eight

Farrakhan Speaks

more like yourself. You register and get them to register. Well how should I register? Should I register as a Democrat? Should I register as a Republican? Should I register as independent? If you're an independent, that's fine. If you're a Democrat, that's fine. If you're a Republican, that's OK. Because in local elections you have to do that which is in the best interest of your local community. But what we want is not necessarily a third party, but a third force. Which means that we're going to collect Democrats, Republicans and independents around an agenda that is in the best interest of our people. And then all of us can stand on that agenda and in 1996, whoever the standard bearer is for the Democratic Party, the Republican Party, or the

Farrakhan Speaks

independent party should one come into

existence. They've got to speak to our agenda.

We're no longer going to vote for somebody just

because they're Black. We tried that. We wish

we could. But we got to vote for you, if you are

compatible with our agenda. Now many of the

people that's in this House right here are put

there by the margin of the Black vote. So in the

next election, we want to see who in here do we

want to stay and who in here do we want to go.

And we want to show them that never again will

they ever disrespect the Black community. We

must make them afraid to do evil to us and think

they can get away with it. We must be prepared

to help them if they're with us or to punish them

if they're against us. And when they're against

Farrakhan Speaks

us, I'm not talking about color. I'm talking about
an agenda that's in the best interest of the
Black, the poor and the vulnerable in this
society. Now atonement goes beyond us. I don't
like this squabble with the members of the
Jewish community. I don't like it. The honorable
Elijah Muhammad said in one of his writings that
he believed that we would work out some kind
of an accord. Maybe so. Reverend Jackson has
talked to the 12 presidents of Jewish
organizations and perhaps in the light of what
we see today, maybe it's time to sit down and
talk. Not with any preconditions. You got pain.
Well, we've got pain, too. You hurt. We hurt, too.
The question is: if the dialogue is proper then
we might be able to end the pain. And ending

Farrakhan Speaks

the pain may be good for both and ultimately
good for the nation. We're not opposed to sitting
down. And I guess if you can sit down with
Arafat where there are rivers of blood between
you–why can't you sit down with us and there's
no blood between us. You don't make sense not
to dialogue. It doesn't make sense. Well,
brothers, I hope Father Clemons spoke today. Is
Father Clemons here? Father Clemons. Do you
know Father Clemons? He is one of the great
pastors. Father Clemons, I wanted him to speak
today because he has a program that he wants
everyone of us when we leave here to go to
some jail or prison and adopt one inmate for the
rest of his and your life to make them your
personal friend–to help them through their

Farrakhan Speaks

incarceration, to be encouragement for them. The brothers who are locked down inside the walls need us on the outside and we need them on the inside. So if every one of us will pick out one inmate, Father Clemons will do the work of guiding this development, because it is his idea, and it is a good idea and the national African-American leadership summit adopts that idea. Thank you, Father Clemons. Will you do that, brothers? How many of you will adopt one Black man in prison and make him your pal, your brother for life. Help him through the incarceration. Well, go to the chaplain of that jail and say, you want to adopt one inmate to start writing to that person, visiting that person, helping that person. And since so many of us

Farrakhan Speaks

have been there already, we know what they

suffer. Let's help our brothers and sisters who

are locked down. Did anybody mention the

political prisons? Brother Conrad Worrell

mentioned our political prisoners, never forget

them. And now, brothers, there are 25,000

Black children in need of adoption. This is our

brother Eason who is the president of Blacks in

Government. I'm sorry, brother Dunston, the

president of the Black Social Workers. He has

25,000 children in need of adoption. Out of this

vast audience, there must be 25,000 men who

will take one of these children and take them

through life and make life worth living for those

children. In this vast audience, is there anyone

one, two, ten, twenty-five, hundred, a thousand,

Farrakhan Speaks

25 thousand who would be willing to adopt a
Black brother or sister, bring them into your
home and rear them properly? How many of you
think you would like to do that, would you just
raise your hand, let me take a look. Raise them
high. That's a wonderful expression. Where
should they do, what should they do, who
should they see? Brothers, the last thing we
want to say, we want to develop an economic
development fund. Suppose, the nearly 2 million
here, and 10 million more back home that
support us gave $10 a month to a national
economic development fund. Inside of one
month, we would have over $100 million. And in
one year, we would have $1.2 billion. What will
we do with that? I would love for the leadership

Farrakhan Speaks

up here to form a board and call in Myrlie Evers Williams and ask her, what is the budget of the NAACP for this year? It's $13 million. It's $15 million, write a check. Now, next year you have to become accountable to the board, and the members of the NAACP will be on the board too, which means that no Black organization will be accountable to anybody outside of us. But accountable to us and we will free the NAACP, the Urban League and all Black organizations to work in the best interest of our people. How many of you would like to see all our Black organizations free? Now, look brothers, an economic development fund for $10 a month is not a big price to ask to begin to build an economic infrastructure to nurture businesses

Farrakhan Speaks

within the Black community. Soon the
leadership is going to meet and work out the
details of an Exodus, Exodus Economic Fund.
And we're going to get back to you. This is not a
one day thing. A task force will be formed right
out of this leadership to make sure that the
things that we say today will be implemented so
that next year on the day of atonement, which
this will take place each and every year from
now on until God says, well done. Now, you saw
the money that was taken up today, didn't you?
How many of you gave some money today? I
see some hands that wanted to give, but didn't
get that box to them. Well, let me tell you
something brothers, we want an outside
accounting firm to come in and scrutinize every

Farrakhan Speaks

dollar that was raised from your pockets to make the Million Man March a success. And if there is any overage, it will not be spent. We will come back to this board of leadership and we will account for every nickel, every dime every dollar. Do you know why? We want Willie Lynch to die a natural death. And the only way we can kill the idea of Willie Lynch, we have to build trust in each other. And the only way we can build trust is to open up the coat and show that you don't have a hidden agenda. All of us will be looking at the same thing, for the same purpose. And then we'll come back to you and make a full accounting for every nickel, every dime and every dollar so that you can trust. I put my life on this. To rob you is a sin. To use you and

Farrakhan Speaks

abuse you is a sin. To make mockery of your love and your trust is a sin. And we repent of all sin and we refuse to do sin anymore. Is that agreeable, Black man? Lord knows if we could do it with blood between us, God knows that Bloods and Crips have done it and what we have done to one another, don't let the sun set before saying to your brother, I love you and I'm sorry. And after the prayer is said and the song is sung, I want you all to just embrace each other and say to each other, I love you my brother and thank you for making this holy day of atonement real in my life. Don't do it now, wait 'til after prayer and the song. Will you bow your heads, please? Oh, before we say that prayer, the brother of my leader and teacher,

Farrakhan Speaks

the honorable Elijah Muhammad, is here with me and with us. He's like my father in the absence of my father. He knows this history of the Nation of Islam better than any man in America and I thank God that he lived long enough to see the day that he suffered and worked for, for now 65 years. The brother of the honorable Elijah Muhammad, brother John Muhammad. We thank you, oh, Allah, for bringing us safely over the highways and we beg you to take us safely back to our wives and our children and our loved ones, who saw us off earlier or a few days ago. And as we leave this place, let us be resolved to go home to work out this Atonement and make our communities a decent, whole, and safe place to live. And oh,

Farrakhan Speaks

Allah, we beg your blessings on all who participated, all who came that presented their bodies as a living sacrifice, holy and acceptable as their reasonable service. Now, let us not be conformed to this world, but let us go home transformed by the renewing of our minds and let the idea of atonement ring throughout America. That America may see that the slave has come up with power. The slave has been restored, delivered, and redeemed. And now call this nation to repentance. To acknowledge her wrongs. To confess, not in secret documents called classified, but to come before the world and the American people as the Japanese prime minister did and confess her faults before the world because her sins have affected the whole world. And perhaps, she may do some act of atonement, that you may forgive and those ill-affected may forgive, that reconciliation and restoration may lead us to the perfect union with thee and with each other. We ask all of this in your Holy and Righteous Name. Allahu, akbar [audience responds: "Allahu, akbar"]. Allahu, akbar ["allahu, akbar"]. Allahu, akbar ["allahu, akbar"]. That means God is great.

Farrakhan Speaks

MIKAZUKI PUBLISHING HOUSE™

(U.S.P.T.O. Serial Number 85705702)

1. 25 Principles of Martial Arts
2. 25 Principles of Strategy
3. American Antifa
4. American Bookstore Directory
5. Arctic Black Gold
6. Art of War
7. Back to Gold
8. Basketball Team Play Design Book
9. Bernie Sanders Revolution
10. Boxing Coloring Book
11. California's Next Century 2.0
12. Camping Survival Handbook
13. Captain Bligh's Voyage
14. Coming to America Handbook
15. Customer Sales Organizer
16. DIY Comic Book
17. DIY Comic Book Part II
18. Economic Collapse Survival Manual
19. Farrakhan Speaks
20. Find The Ideal Husband
21. Football Play Design Book
22. Freakshow Los Angeles
23. Game Creation Manual
24. George Washington's Farewell Address
25. GhostHuntTV Ghost Hunting Notebook
26. Hagakure
27. History of Aliens

Farrakhan Speaks

28. Hollywood Talent Agency Directory
29. I Dream in Haiku
30. Internet Connected World
31. Irish Republican Army Manual of Guerrilla Warfare
32. Japan History Coloring Book
33. John Locke's 2nd Treatise on Civil Government
34. Karate 360
35. Learning Magic
36. Living the Pirate Code
37. Magic as Science and Religion
38. Magicians Coloring Book
39. Make Racists Afraid Again
40. Master Password Organizer Handbook
41. Mikazuki Jujitsu Manual
42. Mikazuki Political Science Manual
43. MMA Coloring Book
44. Mythology Coloring Book
45. Mythology Dictionary
46. Native Americana
47. Ninja Style
48. Ouija Board Enigma
49. Palloncino
50. Political Advertising Manual
51. Quotes Gone Wild
52. Rappers Rhyme Book
53. Saving America
54. Self-Examination Diary
55. Shinzen Karate

Farrakhan Speaks

Facebook.com/MikazukiPublishingHouse

Farrakhan Speaks

KAMBIZ MOSTOFIZADEH TITLES
1. 25 Principles of Martial Arts
2. 25 Principles of Strategy
3. American Antifa
4. American Bookstore Directory
5. Arctic Black Gold
6. Back To Gold
7. Camping Survival Handbook
8. Economic Collapse Survival Manual
9. Find the Ideal Husband
10. Game Creation Manual
11. GhostHuntTV Ghost Hunting Notebook
12. History of Aliens
13. Hollywood Talent Agency Directory
14. Internet Connected World
15. Karate 360
16. Learning Magic
17. Magic as Science & Religion
18. Make Racists Afraid Again
19. Mikazuki Jujitsu Manual
20. Mikazuki Political Science Manual
21. Mythology Dictionary
22. Native Americana
23. Ninja Style
24. Ouija Board Enigma
25. Political Advertising Manual
26. Saving America
27. Small Arms & Deep Pockets
28. Shinzen Karate
29. The Bribe Vibe

Farrakhan Speaks

Facebook.com/KambizMostofizadeh

www.ingramcontent.com/pod-product-compliance
Lightning Source LLC
Chambersburg PA
CBHW060854280326
41934CB00007B/1050